I'm Not An Actor,
(I Just Play One On TV*)

by

dave e. keliher

* a creative memoir

Published by Free The Pig

©2016 Free The Pig (dave keliher)
front & back cover photos by me, too.

the title of this book was suggested by Kathryn Ing. i am dedicating this book to her, and to my parents Patricia and Evan Keliher, and to the many cats i have met, and Humphrey the pig. there are many others i would like to thank and or mention but if i did it would take so long i would never have any time to actually write anything.
and that would suck.

Library of Congress Control Number: 2016901704

Table of Contents

this was gonna be the introduction 1
I'm Not An Actor (I Just Play One On TV) 2
Beginnings 3
Calico The Cat Was Family 5
America: Land of the Free? 7
Guns In My Face 10
A Boy Named Sally 15
phone cable net 22
the last page 25
feed them on your dreams 28
way down below the ocean, that's where i want to be,
    she may be 33
father's day 35
Lost Loves 36
A Brief Investigation: The Life Of a Book Rep 39
Predator and Pray 43
The Lower Level 46
Angel 52
Voices In My Head 55
hitchhiking (there was a time...) 57
Unnecessary Notice 64
The Magic Hat 65

i heard someone call my name 67
A Story of Love.. 69
On A Mission To A Mission To Cover A Fiscal Omission 71
lucky strike 73
Crazy 77
Erin Cat's Tale.. 78
The Chocolate Heart.. 87
the bus waits for no one 99

this was gonna be the introduction

i was going to start this book with an introduction but knew if many people were like me they'd do what i did and skip the intro.

if i did write an intro i would write that yeah, this book is for my parents and kat and cats but it's also for those who lie in bed at night or day and think about all those who have no roof overhead, little or no food in their stomachs, or those who have food and shelter but worry about the disappearing habitats of the elephants and armenian vipers, or those who are angry with the oil industry for hiding their climate change data as they spend the dark hours of their lives finding ways to get their product to market as all the flora and fauna die a slow, painful death.

this is not for those of you who knew what you wanted to do and succeed in doing it, lucky you. (don't be greedy.)

but this was mostly written for those who do not know what to do, or how to do it. and it was written for those who know what to do, know how to do it, but the weight of living in our "survival of the fittest" world is too much…who just wanted to get through the morning, day, and night living in peace and harmony, doing no harm and leaving this world better off than when they arrived. they just want to survive and live good lives without being harassed, ridiculed, abused, starved, broken and imprisoned. this is for you.

and agnostic that i am, and having tremendous doubts there will be anything beyond the end of the road, i do hope and pray as only an agnostic can that there is a heaven above that will provide us all a pain-free world with unconditional love for all that is animate or inanimate and we can do as mr. rodney king asked and "get along."

I'M NOT AN ACTOR
(I JUST PLAY ONE ON TV)

Edgar Lee Master's wrote his *Spoon River Anthology* years before I drew my first breath. If you have not been so lucky to have read this work, what you have missed are a series of tales told by the voices of the dead in a small town cemetery.

The reason I mention this is because I have struggled to tell my story. Though not yet dead, I have spent over fifty years attempting to express myself through the written word and I still have not found my voice. At least I didn't think I had but a few years ago I took another look at my notes and journals and poems and short pieces. And it occurred to me that these pieces are like epitaphs of my own life. Each is part of me, some long buried, others only recently laid to rest. And like the whole of Edgar's *Anthology* which tells the story of one town—my tales taken together tell the story of one man.

In my cemetery, each epitaph was born of and died with me, and though cast into separate graves that appear independent of those that lay nearby, still they share the same ground, same earth, same soul.

Beginnings

In 1884 my great-grandfather was the grocer and mayor of Sault Saint Marie. Sault is pronounced "Soo" which is French for leap which is what the waters would do if they did not pass through the lockes. The Sault is on the northern tip of Michigan on the southern shore of Lake Superior. My great-grandfather had a store there and one winter's day while looking for my voice, I went to find his store but it was gone. I did find the lot where it once stood. It was a nice looking lot so I took a photo which I still have but don't know where it is.

My great-grandfather had money. How much was earned legally through the sale of goods and how much from graft I do not know. But his efforts did allow him to purchase many carriages and horses and homes—though not so many that he lost count. In addition to his material wealth, he had many good Catholic babies and it is possible he would have loved hip hop if he knew he could make a buck off it.

One of my relatives wrote a story about my famous great-grandfather. And between the lines of this piece that placed him on the road to sainthood, I read about my great-grandmother who would never win a Mother-of-the-Year award.

Note: I believe one should be careful about casting stones. Until I can walk on water I am careful about stone-throwing. And I respect how difficult it is to be a mom. If kids knew what responsible parents give up in order to provide for their children this world would be a lot better off. With that in mind...

Granny had lots of babies. (It was god's plan.) And one of them was ill so the doctor said, "This little crapper needs fresh air! Take him to the shores of the Pacific and see if that will cure him."

And so she did. She bundled her baby and many more of her brood and her carriages and horses and whatnots and put them on a train and went Greely-like westward. And when she got there, the baby was healed by the bank of the mighty Los Angeles River.

So she bundled her baby and brood and headed back to the Sault. And as they disembarked the train the baby coughed so they boarded the train and returned to the west.

There.

Now as I was saying, without trying to make this any longer than necessary and without losing sight of my intention to prove whether not-so-great-granny was not so-right-in-the-head, let me cut to the chase.

Granny made so many trips back and forth that she ran out of money. In the meantime, the first seven of her progeny had benefited from the family wealth. They had all gone to college and had good jobs and 401k's. But there were two siblings left: a boy named Evan C. and a girl named Ethel. Granny told the older children,

"Hey, I don't have any money to send Evan and Ethel to school. What am I gonna do?"

And the seven siblings sang to her in unison, "Fuck 'em!"

And so with that, Evan C., my grandfather, had to go to work selling newspapers at the age of nine because they were all too selfish to share what they had with their own blood. And that was how my family had risen from the slums of County Cork to the pinnacle of Sault Saint Marie and slipped to the slums of Detroit.

I guess after reading this over a few times maybe not ALL of the fault lies with Great Granny. Yeah, she could have used a money-manager (one of those that charge a flat rate, not a percentage). But a good portion of the hardship that befell the last two children lands in the laps of their siblings. Fuck them too.

And with that, my story begins.

Calico The Cat Was Family

On Saturday my cat was put to sleep. I know we had her killed; she had a cancer and was in pain. And it was going to get worse.

The night before I threw her a catnip party. And I gave her a midnight dinner. And I cried.

I'm not a very religious person. Never baptized, I would like to be an atheist but there's no way of really knowing.

My parents brought her back from the veterinarian while I was at work.

When I came home she was waiting for me in a box.

I carried her in the box to a hole that I had dug earlier in the day while she was still alive. She was a heavy cat, but never as heavy as she was now. I opened the box. She was curled up, eyes partially open. She was soft as I took her out. I stroked her fur. Yes, soft.

I wrapped her in a white shirt of mine, placed her in the hole, then covered her with some dirt.

A neighbor walked over and asked me if I was planting flowers.

"No," I said, "I'm burying a cat."

"A cat?" (He seemed surprised.)

"Yeah, she had a cancer or something."

(Silence.)

"Fourteen years old."

"Fourteen" he repeated and then he said something or other and moved off.

I was sad.

I wanted to read something to her but I didn't know what. Something I believed in, she believed in. Not the Bible. She wasn't very religious either.

So I read to her from T.S. Eliot's *The Wasteland.*

"In this decayed hole among the mountains,
In the faint moonlight, the grass is singing

> Over the tumbled graves, about the chapel
> There is the empty chapel, only the wind's home.
> It has no windows, and the door swings,
> Dry bones can harm no one.
> Only a cock stood on the rooftree…
> In a flash of lightning. Then a damp gust
> Bringing rain."

Then I closed the book, and covered her with hands full of sorrow and earth. I knew I'd never see her again.

But as I scattered the twigs and leaves over her, I felt I could understand the pain felt by a man burying his child fifty thousand years ago. Though it was a private feeling, there was something universal in its depth, breadth.

Then the feeling faded and I was again alone.

With my cat who had died.

And I was sad,

Very sad.

America: Land of the Free?

Once upon a time, in a land far, far away, a child was born. It was the winter of the Cold War and President Eisenhower was on America's televisions warning the people about the true threat from within—that by the Military Industrial Complex.

Other than that, this land far away was a wondrous place to this newborn. A land where white men of European lineage prospered and also provided a cornucopia of goods and services for them and their families.

But as this child grew and flourished in the 1960's there was something stirring in the consciousness of America. Not all, of course. America would always have more than its share of morons. But many knew change for the better was coming. And this child—let's call him Dave for lack of creativity on the author's part—would sense early on that something was amiss in the land of plenty.

Dave was nine years old when Dr. King was shot outside a hotel in Memphis. But there was no mention of this by Johnny Quest or Haj. And the Banana Splits also failed to proclaim that a great man lay bleeding to death on a passageway outside Room 306. And so this historic moment passed him by.

And when Robert Kennedy was shot at so close a range he could smell the powder from the handgun that took his life, Arnold the Pig from *Green Acres* did not tell Dave, but kept his sadness about the loss to himself. And since Dave's television friends did not tell him that life was terribly unfair, Dave spent much of his early life ignorant of this fact. But he did begin to notice the smaller injustices.

Ramsay suffered from one of those.

Ramsay
Fifth grade. With two parents providing clothing, food, shelter,

love and a boatload of G.I. Joes, what could be wrong with this world? With guitar lessons, judo lessons, swimming lessons, and membership at the local YMCA, how could life not be good?

Fifth grade and Ramsay would provide one answer.

Fifth grade and a playground and recess.

Recess. Can you remember recess? You work your ass off, or not, and then the bell rings and the teacher says go outside and play. Go kick a ball, race your friends, jump a rope. When is the last time your supervisor blew a whistle and told you to go play?

Recess. We played. We yelled. We ran and pushed and laughed.

Kickball, tetherball, monkey bars and jacks.

And then I saw Ramsay.

I don't know why I stopped. I had seen Ramsay before. Many times seen him standing there. And I never stopped.

But this time I did.

Ramsay stood alone.

Ramsay stood against the wall.

The wall didn't move and neither did he.

And the rest of the children swirled all about.

Full of life and hope and...

Ramsay stood against the wall.

And I was stopped and standing not far from Ramsay. And I looked at him and he looked different this day. But he wasn't different. I was. And I watched him. And he watched the other children. But they did not see him. And in his eyes I saw hope. Hope that maybe someone would approach him and say, "Hello Ramsay." But no one did, not even me because I was only ten and who was I to change the way things were? But I did recognize that he should not be standing alone when he wanted his life to be more than what it was. That was wrong. Unjust.

But where did this come from? What or who would allow this feeling of hope in a ten-year-old child to be unfulfilled? Was this self-inflicted, learned, a genetic mutation? I didn't know then and

I don't know today.

And then the bell rang. And we ran inside. And though I left Ramsay standing alone, I have not forgotten him. Because of him I had, at that moment, begun to wonder why I had so much—and others so little.

And this would lead to questions that no words from any books or beings, dead or alive, have fully answered. But it doesn't mean I didn't start to form a partial answer. That day made me aware there are many Ramsays in this world; people who don't feel like they belong. We should let them know they are not alone, invisible, but are real and part of this crazy world because at one point we are all Ramsays. And it's important that we acknowledge this and stop and say, "Hello" to the Ramsays of this world.

And that is what I have tried to do

to this very day.

GUNS IN MY FACE

Gun One

The first time I had a gun in my face it seemed, at the time, to mean nothing. Just a gun in the face. Neither good nor bad—just there.

I had gone to Mary's. Everyone I knew who was anybody went to Mary's. At least anybody who wanted to get high went there. And that's what we did and had been doing since the beginning of 7th grade. And now, two years later, as my friend Mark and I entered the house the front door shut fast behind us and we turned to see the Doh brothers. The Doh brothers were sociopathic. I didn't know that word at the time. But I knew something was really fucking wrong with them. Da Doh was standing with his back to the door and pointing a shotgun at our heads.

12 gauge pump.

I just stood there looking at them: the Doh brothers and the gun.

But I knew they weren't going to shoot. I knew it the same way a sixteen year-old in his '67 Z/28 Camaro can push his speedometer to three figures on a dead end street and know he won't die.

Mick Doh, the younger of the two, laughed. And then Da did, too, and lowered the barrel toward the ground.

"You got any guns?" Da asked.

"We're going hunting," added Mick.

Sociopaths with guns running around the woods of Michigan didn't really seem to faze me. It happened every hunting season. Two more wouldn't make a difference.

"My dad's got a shotgun," I said.

You know what I find is really interesting about people—how fucking stupid they can be. Why the hell would I tell sociopaths who are looking for a gun that my dad had one? But it just came out.

"You think we can borrow it?" asked Da.

"No, probably not."

"Fuck," said Mick.

But they pretty much let the whole thing drop and we left, heads intact.

Gun Two

A friend of mine, let's call him Eric because that's his name, came to visit from Colorado. We had gone to elementary school together so we had known each other for quite some time. I picked him up at his parent's house and we drove over to an indoor theater in Dearborn. The main entrance was on Michigan Avenue with some parallel parking out front but mostly people parked in the large lot to the rear. We were visiting Lori, a friend of ours who managed the theater. While standing in the lobby chatting with her I noticed two guys had positioned themselves at the front doors, sitting on either side on the floor. I don't know why I noticed them. They didn't seem to be doing anything out of the ordinary. But there was something about them that made me wonder why they were there.

After a short visit we headed out the doors that were now clear and walked around the block to the rear. As we approached the car I heard someone yell. It had been dark and cold and overcast and somehow I had failed to notice that the two sentries I had seen earlier had become twelve and were coming toward us from all over and yelling at us. I didn't know what was up but I knew I didn't have a lot of time to think. I grabbed Eric and shoved him back toward where we had come from and I followed him as we raced toward the building with the angry pricks in pursuit. When we got to the wall we went right and as we ran a metal pipe flew past my head and bounced and rattled on the ground in front of me.

I stopped and picked it up and turned on the pricks and began to yell,

"WHAT THE FUCK DO YOU WANT??!!" which I repeated

because I didn't know what else to ask until they at least answered that.

By now they had stopped and were closing in.

And then I heard a new voice yell from behind,

"Drop the pipe!"

I turned and there was a man with a gun standing there and he was pointing it at me and I didn't want to drop the pipe. And he yelled,

"Drop the pipe!"

And I looked at the gun which he was holding with two hands and pointing at my face.

Eric told me to drop the pipe.

And so I did and I found out the gunman was an undercover cop.

Who says there aren't happy endings?

The cops had been watching the lot because these pricks had been gathering but the cops didn't know why. They just knew something was up and we became bait.

What's different about this gun as opposed to the previous was that I had left my Camaro/dead-end-street state of mind long ago and knew this time I was this close to being the subject of one of those two paragraph stories in section B of the local paper. It would have followed the one of the couple being run over by a bus.

Gun Three

Even though I spent most of my life in the suburbs of Detroit, a girlfriend of mine and I did spend a few years living near 7 Mile and Gratiot in an upstairs flat; her mom lived downstairs on the main floor. Rita, the girlfriend, had grown up there and had for years felt comfortable walking about. But the streets had changed and even her comfort level had diminished.

The prostitute woke us up at three a.m. banging on the door because some john was pissed he hadn't gotten what he paid for. I, born and bred in the suburbs, was going to open the door to help this damsel when Rita screamed to "keep the fucking door closed!" I could see the john in his car in our driveway yelling "bitch" before he backed off and sped away. Yeah, it was a short time later I purchased my own Mossberg 12 gauge pump and had a friend in the Fire Protection business set us up with a house alarm.

The upper and lower flats shared a common entryway. When you entered you had ten-seconds to deactivate the alarm. Now, if we came home and Mom wasn't in, we'd deactivate it and then after stepping onto the stairs, reactivate it so that it was still active when Mom came home. Got that?

But sometimes we might forget to reactivate and Mom would come home and, being hard of hearing, wouldn't notice there was no warning sound and reactivate it thinking we had activated it. What she really did was turn it on which we would all learn two minutes later when she would set it off by walking around her place.

Anyway, one day we came home and Mom wasn't in so we set the alarm and went upstairs. And a while later the alarm rang out like a macaw greeting an unwelcome visitor.

We waited figuring Mom would turn it off and we'd go back to sleep.

But the macaw kept screaming.

So we waited a while longer. Then we called her phone downstairs. No answer. And the alarm seemed to be getting louder.

Did I mention I purchased a shotgun?

I told Rita,

"I'm gonna go downstairs and see what the problem is. If there is someone down there and they grab me, you shoot 'em."

I don't know if I had been watching too many Laurel and Hardy movies or what. And we hadn't been getting along that well at the time. I don't know if she really didn't love me anymore because she readily agreed to the plan.

I opened the door.

I started down the stairs.

She stepped onto the landing and pointed the gun in the direction of where the attack was anticipated.

When I got halfway down I looked back at her and realized I was fucked. I mean, the stairwell was pretty narrow. When (if?) I got to the bottom and Charles Manson grabbed me, there would be two bodies lying on the lower landing.

I continued down and when I got to bottom I turned off the alarm and luckily there was no one in the house. The next day I brought up the fact my plan to take out Manson was seriously flawed.

"Yeah," she said.

If there is one thing I've learned from this it's to avoid guns in your face. And if you're going to argue with someone, don't hand her a gun afterwards.

A Boy Named Sally

Walter Gabrini was my mother's father. By day Walter was a City of Detroit Boiler Operator and licensed by the state to test other operators so they too could be licensed so as to not blow boilers to bits.

By night he, Walter, was a very talented woodworker.

Made all kinds of stuff.

Little whirligigs and doodads and whatnots. I still have a whatnot which sits over my desk: a wooden catboat he made in nineteen forty when he was quarantined in the hospital with tuberculosis. The boat is an assemblage of hand-carved planks and slats that he heated and bent along the frame to form the flare, sheer, and tumblehome. It's a beautiful boat, two feet long with a mast three feet high and though it didn't look like the one Humphrey Bogart sailed in *To Have and Have Not* it did look like one he might have wanted to.

I always admired Walter's work and thought I might have the same hands and skill. In sixth grade Woodshop chance walked in the door and said, "Show me." Chance, in the guise of Mr. Fritzie, the Shop teacher, provided us with the opportunity to work with an electric lathe. Every student was given a block of wood four inches square and twelve inches in length.

Mr. Fritzie said to the class,

"Thinka the possibilities! If you could make anything in the world, what would you make?"

I looked down at the wood before me. Not a freakin' clue.

Fritzie continued. "If Jesus were to appear before you, what do you think He would have you make?"

I raised my hand.

"Yeah Sally, whatizit?"

He called me Sally. You know, looking back that doesn't seem like a great idea. I mean, Johnny Cash had his *Boy Named*

Sue who learned to take a beating, then give one in turn. But that wouldn't happen to me. I had braces on my teeth. Braces don't make a good fighter, just a bloody mess. The first day in class Fritzie looked at my hair and he just started calling me Sally. Hell, I couldn't blame him. My hair went all the way down to my collar which was a revolutionary look for a sixth grader in the suburbs of the Motor City in nineteen seventy.

I said, "Wasn't Jesus a fisherman? I mean, that was his thing. Son of God and a fisherman. I know they say He was a carpenter but I never read anywhere where they talked about Him building a picnic table or gazebo or carving a bear out of a tree stump. You would think if He did a bear like that they would have written about it. I mean, they bragged about Him catching a shit load of fish and multiplying them like a fish farm in Puget Sound, but nada a word about him and his wood."

"Did you say 'shit'? God damn it how many times do I have to tell you we don't say 'shit' in this class." He threw a chalkboard eraser at me and it bounced off my head leaving a white streak down my center part. That shut me up.

"Let us pray for guidance," Fritzie said and the class bowed their heads and prayed. Instead of looking down I kept my head up and my eyes open because my old man told me that when a preacher tells you to bow your head that's when your shit's sure to disappear. But instead of just eyeballing Fritzie I found myself looking up to the ceiling or possibly the heavens and asking, "What the hell am I gonna do with my wood?"

That's when I saw the light.

I mean literally saw the light. I should make a light bulb.

God wanted me to make a light bulb out of wood. And this was quite a revelation for an agnostic. My first connection to God.

I made a sketch and showed it to Fritzie and he looked at it and said, "Whatizit?"

"It's a light bulb."

He wasn't sold. "When I told you to pray, did you?"

"Yeah."

"And God told you to make a light bulb?"

"Yeah."

He looked at me. "Sally, what church do you go to?"

"I don't go to church."

He smiled and nodded his head. "I see. I didn't know you were a heathen. If I had known…" He shook his head and then he looked at me again. "You go make your light bulb, son," and he put his hand on my shoulder, "and you keep praying."

"Thanks!"

So I went to work. And for the next five weeks I turned and shaped and sanded and shellacked and buffed that piece of wood and felt as close to heaven as I would probably ever get.

And when I finished I gave it to my father on Father's Day.

He said, "Nice, where are the others?"

"Others? What others?"

"It's a bowling pin, right? Shouldn't there be ten?" he asked.

"It's a light bulb."

"But it's wood."

"Yeah. I made it in Shop Class. You know, woodworking. See the threads. It's supposed to be screwed in."

"Will it light up?" He appeared to really like that idea and brightened at the thought.

Maybe I was adopted. "No, it's a wooden light bulb."

He dimmed.

"I guess it is," he said.

Lights out.

I showed it to Grandpa Walter.

"Where are the others?" he asked.

Even though my woodworking days were pretty much over, I did have one more opportunity to shine.

A Volcano And My Pants

In seventh grade the students of Haston Middle School were "encouraged" to enter the science fair or fail. Luckily Mr. Fritzie wasn't around to tell me to look to Jesus for ideas. I mean, maybe if Jesus were alive today he would be working at Home Depot and selling lumber like there was no tomorrow, and He would know that better than anybody.

But I had read the Bible and knew damn well He should not be teaching science. Hell, on the very first page of the Bible Jesus puts the earth at the center of the universe. Wouldn't you think that if you MADE the universe you would remember where you put Earth?

Unless you were busy. I know I've made things and forgotten where I put them. But how could He lose us?

Wait, maybe that's the problem!

God made us and then forgot where he put us. You can't blame Him. I'll just say that when He gets back to us and finds out what we've done to this planet He's gonna kick some royal ass. But I'm not worried—I'll tell him, "Don't blame me, I recycle!" Let's see how he gets around that.

I tried to come up with a project and couldn't come up with squat. My mom, who was a librarian and always full of some fun fact said volcanoes were cool.

And so I decided to make a volcano. (Sometimes life can be simple.)

Now it wasn't going to be the traditional flour and oil mess with baking soda spewing out like some newborn rejecting lunch. Mom wasn't going to have a mess in her house. I wasn't sure of my next step so Mom called Grandpa Walter up and told him I needed to make a science fair project. He came over to the house and we went to my father's office and laid out some drafting paper and a T-square and he started to sketch this real cool volcano. But it was rather complex.

"It looks rather complex," my Dad said.

"Christ all mighty, I could whip this thing up in no time past seven. That's how kids win the ribbons, you know? Let the adults do it. How much of this does he really need to do?" asked the Walt.

"As much as possible," Dad said. Sometimes my father had too much integrity, which really can get on one's nerves. Did you ever meet someone with integrity? Can piss you off after a while. Who do they think they are?

Walter looked over at the wooden light bulb on Dad's desk and nodded his head. He took the drawing he had made and ripped it from the board and began again.

My volcano was a flat wooden box with an image of a volcano painted on it revealing various strata. But the topper was the Christmas lights affixed so that when you pushed a button in the legend the appropriate lights would illuminate. Yeah, it was something I did with my own two hands.

And it sucked.

On Science Fair Day the teacher escorted us to the gymnasium where we looked for the winners and losers. Winners had ribbons. Losers had nothing.

I found my volcano and it was ribbonless. No shit, Sherlock.

I did notice that the extension cord I had purchased from the D&C Drugstore was no longer connected to my volcano but was now connected to a strange project illustrating how DNA was passed from parent to child. But instead of using fruit flies or mice the student had taken 3D models of Frankenstein and the Bride of Frankenstein, each bound to their own miniature gurney, and showed how if they had a child he would look something like Richard Nixon.

There was no ribbon here, either. But the reason they had taken my extension cord was to power the small lights strategically placed so that when you pressed a button a series of lights would flow from Frankie's privates to hers and when you pushed another button the Mrs. had lights in her breasts that would flash. And as I was about to push another button Mr. Brown, another science teacher, approached.

I thought he had come over to admire the lights. Instead he said to me,

"Excuse me, but you're not supposed to be wearing pants."

Now that was unexpected.

I was only thirteen years old and really hadn't been around the world a long time or traveled far. I mean, Alison Z. and I had spent time in her basement exploring new ways to play Twister but we had kept our clothes on and as Harry Chapin said, the lessons hadn't gotten very far.

I said to Mr. Brown the Clown, "Say what?"

"You're not supposed to be wearing pants."

To have Mr. Brown the science clown approach me in broad daylight and tell me I shouldn't be wearing pants did kinda freak me out. I just thought I didn't hear him right.

But he repeated it twice more. And there were others who heard him. A crowd was gathering. And he didn't seem to care. I thought, how fucking brazen?! Is this what life has in store for me? This adult male teacher had the hots for me—of course I couldn't blame him—I did have a certain charisma I knew the world would eventually recognize.

"You're going to have to leave," continued Mr. Clown.

"And go where? Your place?"

"You know that girls aren't allowed to wear pants. It's the rules."

Girl? Who's a girl? Maybe this Sally business had gone too far. I was about ready to call him a perv. How much more of this was I going to have to take? And then Mrs. Poman, my science teacher, appeared like popcorn magic jumping right out of the pan.

She said to the clown, "Mr. Brown."

"Yes?"

"That's a boy."

"What!? No way, she—"

"He's a student of mine. I know."

You bet she knew! She could recognize a man when she saw one.
Mr. Brown didn't know what to say. Hell, neither did I.
Mr. Brown apologized. Damn well he should!

Afterward I did kinda laugh.
It's important to laugh at clowns.
There are enough of them around to make you think the whole world's a circus.

phone cable net

phone bill arrives.
it's too much.
too much money.
too much of a good thing.
asking too much of me.
time to switch.
time to change.
i'd rather switch than fight.
remember that?
corporate ad for death sticks
pounded into my head as a child in the 60s.
while one group fought against the Vietnam debacle
a cig company jumped into a fight of their own
and tried to convince us to fight for our right to die
at an early age.
but how do we let corporations bring our lives
to an early end by feeding us excess sugar,
cholesterol, alcohol, nicotine, gasoline.
and yet when a man in his sixties says
the cancers and parkinson's he received
as an agent orange bonus from fighting in 'Nam
are too much to bare
and now he wants to end his life peacefully
at a time and place he chooses,
surrounded by family and a bowl of
oregon Applesauce,
he is not allowed to do so?
we humans are a crazy mu-fa bunch.

but what about the phone bill?
while death with dignity plays in the rear of
my cerebral cortex I still must face
the thousands of green backs i dish

out yearly for cell phone with the family plan plus
cable or satellite, and a land line in case there is a
quake and I need to reach—who?
all my connections are cell only.
and we can't forget the 'net connection—
as fast as most 3rd world countries
(why should they install fiber when
they make more by giving us less?).

but how to switch?
att v. t mobile v. verizon v. sprint v. virgin.
rollover minutes, activation fees, monthly service,
taxes, admin fees, data usage, hot spots,
text messages and upgrades will cost me more.
but not as much as cancellations.

am I under contract?
is my significant other under contract?
are the kids, cat, dog and grandpa
under contract?
who is eligible to switch?
take our numbers with us.
leave our troubles behind.
find new troubles when we arrive.
coverage area?
weigh all the options.
do a ben franklin close.
flip a coin.
drink a beer.
two out of three.
drink another.
best of five.
play a game of quarters.
drink a beer.
stop.

try to remember what it was i was doing.
look at my phone bill again.
say fuck it
and set up an automatic online payment and
ask not to receive paper copies of my bills so
i never have to look at them again.

grab another beer.
sit back and put on the inDirect tv and watch the
dodgers win the pennant…
but then realize i can't because I don't get the dodgers
cuz direct tv won't agree to choke up a billion cash
so they can pass the tab to me.
i'd rather watch reruns of Kung Fu.

damn, maybe I should cut the cord
and get a roku apple tv chome usb
antenna on the roof what the hell!

have another beer.

the last page

this is the last page.
i'm having difficulty breathing and i think i may be dying.
so if i am i guess i had better write my last page.

last year...or was it the year before?...i had started my memoir.
and now there's a decent chance i won't finish it.
i've written 22 pages.
and that might be all.
fifty-two years old and twenty-two pages. let's see, that's two point three six pages per year.

?
wait. that ain't right. it's point four two pages per year.
per year? dang, it's a good thing i didn't rely solely on my ability to write. maybe i should divide my years by the words i've written? or divide by loves found? loves lost? no, that would be too depressing.
friends made? hugs exchanged...for cash? tears shed?

"sunshine on my shoulders makes me happy..."
        john Denver

those are nice words.
and he died in an ultralight flying over the hills of northern California.
i hope he was happy before the wind cut out.

today.
today i walked to the back of the zoo. it was a blue sky yellow sunny day. and on my way i saw the meerkats standing tall on their rock, the black-necked swans swam with the mallard and his wife, and life was good for me.

so i guess this is a good day to die.
good night kat. i will miss you when i am gone.
and i hope you will know in your heart that you are a very special person and i am lucky to have found you—a flower in the desert, and i tried to be your little prince, to love you and protect you and comfort you.

to my parents…
sorry. i find it difficult to say much more. it's hard to see the words.
there are so many good people i have met.
let's focus on that.
and i hope, really hope, we can do better.
as Murray said in A 1000 Clowns, "People, we need a better class of garbage in the streets."

yeah. put that on my tombstone.
whatever!
love,
davey k.
[note: whoever finds this, add this to the final pieces and publish on kindle.]

I Did Not Die

dear reader:
a few months ago i wrote a piece called "the last page"
when i thought i was having a heart attack and dying.
well, i didn't die.

sometimes i have panic attacks when i think,
what if i fail to die?
i mean, when it's my turn to die,
and i don't.
i just keep on living…

what hell is that?
don't get me wrong. i enjoy many days.
but i'm not interested in going beyond my expiration date.
just wanted to make that clear.

guess i'll add more to my memoir.

"feed them on your dreams"
—graham nash

i was thinking of my father…
he's seventy-nine—half way there, as i say.
i was thinking of my brothers, who we are...
and these thoughts occurred to me…

my father had so many dreams.
had? hah!
my father *has* so many dreams!
he's a dreamer.
he's a dreamer who not only dreams but does
and is still doing.
every day he's still putting pen to paper,
fingers to keyboard,
because he believes, he knows, that his Pulitzer is just
a phone call away…
and Broadway, which is just five and a half hours east,
will soon beckon…

as children he, like most parents who care,
told us his dreams. i see them as a trinity.

the first was wanderlust.
he would tell us of kerouac and kerouac's Road.
and we brothers three would talk about hitting the road,
seeing america from a Harley…
we'd watch "Then Came Bronson" on tv and Pop would tell us
"you know you don't have to get married when you're young…"
as if knowing this would allow us to keep our options open…
free us to see what might be.

my father followed his own road,

leaving home at sixteen to join the Marines,
having to doctor his birth certificate so he could make the cut…
a journey that would take him to south carolina
where he would see the White's Only drinking fountains
and know this was another of a long line of injustices that
had plagued humankind.
the Marines shipped him to san diego where he would see
what life could be like without snow,
then on to guam where he learned on his first day that he could
hold twelve, count them, twelve coconuts in his arms and how
great it felt
and then months later grew weary of
seeing those friggin' seeds everywhere.
he continued west to japan where a fellow Marine,
wounded from the fight in korea, convinced my father he was
missing out by not being in the mix.
so my father transferred from KP duty in japan to end up on
a truck that arrived in time for him to fight in the battle of the
Chosin Reservoir where he and his pals would end up in retreat,
heading south of the 38th parallel and eventually stateside.
valuable lesson learned.

the second dream was more sensible:
seeing that the Marines offered nothing of value but the g.i. bill,
he attended college where he became a history teacher.
a college education can provide a more secure life, he said.
they can't take knowledge away from you.
he did have a minor detour in law school and
though he only spent a few semesters there, he said that law
can open a lot of doors.
he would regale us with his ventures into the business side of
america during his summers off from teaching.
i'm talking *sales*, the blood that pumps capitalism's heart.
he quoted og mandino:
"if you can sell you can make a living anywhere."

it wasn't the willy loman angle.
this was the "take responsibility for yourself,
grab those bootstraps and give a yank and get to it".
despite these diversions, he stuck to his teaching because
not only did it provide for his family but allowed him to pursue
what he was meant to be: a writer.

as a child he learned to love the words of Twain,
Hemmingway, Steinbeck, and Bierce.
and so his third dream was born:
he would find his place among
these literary greats.

so he set to it.
each evening after he returned from school and had dinner with
his family, he retired to his "office" to write.
and write he did:
wonderful stories and plays and scripts for the big screen and small.
stories about his life, though at times stretched a bit.
(he didn't actually help jesus with the Second Advent—at least not yet.)

as children these are the themes we heard,
recounted in variations.

and this is what i have seen:

my eldest brother alan michael's story is
even more entertaining than voltaire's Candide.
but here i will only offer a glimmer.

in nineteen seventy-two when alan was fifteen
he left home for washington d.c. so he could
participate in the march to end the war in vietnam.

he failed to share his itinerary with our parents
who were surprised when alan was not home for
dinner that day.

from d.c. he joined a band of
marchers and went to Boulder where
he hung out until he was arrested for
breaking curfew. he was handcuffed
and put on a plane for Detroit.
(no, that wasn't his punishment, it's where
we lived.)
but he wouldn't stay long.
soon he was off, hitchhiking his way across
the grasslands and mountains to the pacific waters.
that was one of alan's gift—
though at times my parents didn't see it that way—
his ability to leave home with
fifty dollars in his pocket and travel thousands of miles.
eventually he did settle down by the sea in OB
where he lives with his wife—the only woman
in the world who has managed to capture his
heart, and he, hers.

brother brian, the younger, has been the most practical—
a business major-law school grad-family man-homeowner.
he created the Flush Rush Quarterly where he took
Rush Limbaugh to task for being an outrageous
ass. he ran for Congress against a idiot who was lucky
to have in his campaign war chest a quarter mil compared
to my bro brian's ten k.
if it wasn't for that, we'd be calling him congressman keliher.
(perhaps he's better off retaining his honor by not being elected.)
he became a professor of business law—
the nuts don't fall far from the tree…
he is blessed with a lovely family.

and lastly here i am,
lucky in love and life.

in my spare time i look for answers to my questions,
and question my answers,
listen to graham nash and lightfoot,
put fingers to keyboard.

i have written far less than my father.
but that's not the point.
the point is i have a dream.
and it is a dream i received from my father.—
different than those chosen by my brothers.
but the dreams we have chosen keep us alive.
we, the sons of evan keliher,
are survivors
and together, us three,
we are
evan keliher—
a great father, great writer, great man,
loved very much by those who are lucky enough
to have heard him
share his dreams.

good day, father evan,
and good night.

> **way down below the ocean,**
> **that's where i want to be, she may be***
>
> —Donovan Leitch

i wrote the following which is true.
a true story you can *tell* another when you're in
a pub or church or the backseat of a '68 dodge coronet.
but that doesn't mean you can publish it…
this is, if it includes words that were written by someone else,
even if you cite the source.
for example, let's say there was a singer named Donovan.
a gifted writer, tale-teller, a sensitive and caring poet
in his own right.
and let's say in the story i quoted a line from one of his songs.
it's his song. his words. but i quote them.

let's say i reached out to Donovan and asked his people
if i could use the line in my story. and let's say Donovan replied,
through his people to my people,
"no, man. i don't let others do that."

and i respect that.
so i won't use his words in my story.
but i did title this story with words i'm gonna refer to
'cause you can't copyright a title.
so when i say, "title", lift your gaze.

once upon a time when i worked in a cubicle,
the busy season ended and my manger called
us together and said,
"i have evaluation forms i will be distributing
and i want you all to evaluate yourselves."

the forms were passed around.
i went to my hovel and read over the questions.
and as i began to write my answers
i found, to my dismay, i could not
give them what they wanted
because what they wanted was not
being true to who i was,
true to what i felt.

so i asked myself a question:
what did i feel?
and then i answered myself
and i wrote these words:
"*title."
and then i made the proper attribution to Donovan.
and then i handed her the paper and walked away
but i did not get far.
she caught up to me and said,
"i cannot hand this in. you must do it again."

so i took it back to my hovel
and sat upon my chair and reread the questions.
and then i began to write,
"*title."

i wrote that because that was what was real.
and if i could not be real,
then what was i?

i handed my manager the papers once more.
and she looked from me—
to the papers—
and then back at me.
and i smiled as best i could,
and i turned,
and walked
away.

father's day

what can a son say to his father after
fifty-three years?
what can a son say to the man who
gave life,
gave time,
gave love
for so long?

i don't have the words…
but i can say
thank you.
thank you for letting me see
so many wonderful things…
and i will do my best to
do the same for those i meet.
i will take those valuable lessons,
and give to those around me
my time,
my love,
and hope they will do the same
and the chain will remain
unbroken.
that's a legacy worth sharing.

lost loves

i drive the highway.
i see you in your car as i drive past.
you are smoking a cigarette and i say,
"i am better than you.
"i do not smoke.
"i take vitamins and can still wear my velour jacket
from senior high,
with matching pants with flared bells from a time
when they were in fashion and i am better than you are."

light goes red to green and
she is gone.

another light another car.
i look at her, she at me.
i do not know her but what if i did?
what if i knew her and could say to her:
"do you know the feeling i get when i think of your eyes?
it is your eyes i want to see.
i want to see your eyes looking at me.
i want them to sparkle and flash and twinkle-twinkle like stars
from the heavens.
i want to hold you and tell you i love you even though i do not
know who you are.
i want to take you to Zion to spend time with old friends of mine i
have not seen for years.

light goes red to green.

at the seven-11
i saw a woman who purchased only one half gallon of
homogenized three percent fat milk

and i would have asked her out but i cannot deal with that—
three percent fat.
it's just too much.
so i say nothing.

lastly…
to the woman on the phone from the major movie studio which
will remain anonymous per their lawyers request…i say i enjoyed
our verbal flirtations but when i told you my analyst was available
if you cared you said you already had one, thank you very much.

and it was like we had crossed some line and could not go back
because i actually had no analyst and now i know you did and why
did you need one and why should that concern me because most
of us probably should have someone we can trust to talk with us
about all there is and i would sometimes like to do the same but
damn if i'm gonna tell You about it and god forbid my insurance
knows which is why i pay cash and always wear a scarf.

that is, if i Were to go i would do those things but i have no need
to, so there.

actually it was her lack of interest in seeing Chicken Run
that caused the rub.
"is it the clay-mation thing that bothers you?" i ask.
she says "no".
but i can sense there is something else… so i ask,
"is it chickens?"
she says, "no, she loves chickens and will never stop eating them."

never and *stop eating*? (what has that to do with aardman studios?)
"well, once you see Chicken Run you will be eating a lot more
burgers—
at least that's what the chickens hope."
she says, "i will never stop eating chickens. i will take them to my

grave. and besides, chickens have no hope."
"not with you around," i add.
things don't go well after that.

sometimes when i drive fro and to and all about i see the bus-bus-riders and want to give them rides to their destinies but how does one approach them because we in this city are on the defensive if not just down right offensive.

i saw a rider waiting by and by and she was reading a novel which was novel because reading is so important to me and when i think i could just move in with any pretty face and make things work like the Catholics did in the old days (may they rest in peace), but then i realize the dream would come to a quick end when i saw her eyes failed to flicker just so.

light goes red to green
and on i go,
with lost loves into the night.

A Brief Investigation: The Life of a Book Rep
(in One Act)

Date of Inquiries: February 8, a Friday, to February 10, a Sunday, 1985
Settings: Offices of the University of Michigan (Dearborn); Madonna College (Livonia) and a Phone booth on Cass Ave. and 2nd. (Detroit)
Characters in Order of Appearance:

Dave Keliher	The Inquisitor
Dr. R. Wessman	The Engineer
Dr. Kautoroff	The Educator
Mr. Don Lilly	The Bookstore Manager
Dr. Bartholomew	The Economist
Dr. E. Nolan	The English Master
Ms. C. Sullivan	The Book Representative

    The point of this report was to allow myself more insight into the world of book representatives and to find out what impact, if any, they have on professors and bookstore managers.
    These are my observations.

    Dr. Wessman teaches classes in line perspective and projection. I realize this is not a class that is in demand but he was the first person that I could spend some time with. He does not use a textbook for his class and any materials he does use are printed by the University. He is working on a book, has been for the last six years or so.
    He said that he has not seen many book representatives. This may have to do with the fact his classes are not at the freshman level, not to mention the subject matter. He enjoyed talking about his classes and the materials he used in teaching (e.g., the use of transparencies).

It was lunchtime when I finished talking to Dr. Wessman. There were few professors in. Dr. Kautoroff was one of the few I found. She was very busy and said she was running late for a meeting in Grand Rapids. I asked if I could stop back later that day. She said I could try.

A half-hour later I did. I followed her from office to office and asked her questions. She said she liked sales reps in general. They did influence what she selected, "because they know what is new," and she does not. As for positive qualities a rep should "be direct and to the point because professors don't always have a lot of time, and they should be familiar and knowledgeable of the materials."

I thanked her for the information and departed. I walked across the campus to the bookstore and asked for the manager.

"Mr. Lilly? Umm, oh, there he is over there."

I didn't see whom she was referring but walked in the direction she indicated and asked for Mr. Lilly.

"I am Lilly. Could I help you?"

"I'm doing a campus project on the life of a book representative."

"You look like a book rep."

"Thank you." I presumed that was a compliment. Mr. Lilly came forward from behind a counter. I introduced myself and spent the next forty-five minutes listening to him spin delightful and horrifying tales of the book world. In brief, he told me he had little use for book reps. "When I need them," he said, "they ain't there. I call and get a recording. I don't need a recording. So I call directly to the publisher."

So much for book representatives. But he did tell me what happens when books he orders don't show, or the invoices are missing, or the professor dies, or the course is changed and no one tells him so the books sit on the shelf. It was fascinating. I thanked him very much for his time and insights and continued on my way.

A moment later I cornered Dr. Bartholomew. He was smoking his pipe and perusing an Economic text.

"Excuse me," I said, "but I was wondering if you could tell me about book representatives and—"

"HA!" He cut me off mid-sentence. "Book reps. I've got a meeting in five minutes but I'll tell you this: Some of my best friends are reps. The good ones don't give me any shit. You guys act as liaisons between me and the publisher."

"Do reps influence what you select?"

"No. You guys aren't sales so much as you're there to make sure we get the books. Make sure we're happy with 'em. Do we have any problems type stuff. You know?"

"Are there any positive or negative qualities you can think of?"

"Negative? Don't give or feed shit. Don't tell the prof what to take. I had a guy in here arguing with me whether a book was good or not. Don't argue with me. Positive? Show me you care what I think."

"A little Dale Carnegie or common sense."

"Right. But you'd be surprised how many don't have that."

"Is there a rep you can recommend for me to talk to?"

He looked in his desk drawer. "Yeah. Here's one. Colleen," and he gave me her card. "She's good. Well, I gotta be going."

"Thank you very much for your time. I really appreciate it."

"It's okay." We shook hands and he left in a puff of smoke.

The day was passing quickly now. I headed for my daily sales meeting at the MetroVision Cable TV Office where I had to spend some time. As soon as I found an out I took it and checked in with Dr. Nolan at Madonna College. He's the director of the MBA program and influential in the English department.

"Doc. What do you think of book reps?"

"They're a pain in the neck. They drop in without appointments. And then stop back later to see if you've read the books they've dropped off. I often don't have time to read the books. I usually give them to friends to read."

"Do they influence what you buy?"

"No. Not really. I do like the promotional materials they have."

"What characteristics do you like to see?"

"I like it when they call ahead and make appointments. There's also one thing I would like to see in reps."

"What's that?"

"A sense of humor."

And with that I produced my juggling cubes from my bag and juggled while I told him one-liners courtesy of W.C. Fields. He was amused and we had a beer or two to end the night.

Sunday evening I called Colleen Sullivan, a book representative recommended by Dr. Bartholomew. Colleen told me she enjoyed publishing and the responsibility of getting books to the professors because it helped "better service the educational process." She felt she had a substantial amount of influence on her clients, but advised that one "shouldn't tell them what to buy."

As for characteristics, she said, "Don't be overbearing, a know-it-all, or unreceptive. Be pleasant, outgoing, charming."

I thanked her and hung up.

Lights down. A single spot center stage for the Summary.

Summary.

I have learned a lot. I have heard the good and the bad. This job requires someone who is responsible and organized. She should be understanding and concerned about the needs and the wants of her clients and her employer. Common sense and good, sound judgment are integral ingredients in the make-up of a successful and superior book/sales representative.

This job is for someone that possesses these qualities.

This job is for me.

(curtain down)

Note: I did not get the job, and I am a better man for it.

predator and pray

for those of us who do not belong
in a world
where the conflict between
prey and predator
is the norm…

for those of us who wonder why an entity
who possesses all the powers and magic
one could imagine—
and with these tools
creates a world where hunger and pain
and loneliness
are so prevalent,
where inequity is more common than
the fish in the seas…

for those who belong to this group of those
who do not belong
i write these words so that you will know that you
are not alone.
there are many of us—
many who are only connected through
the channeling of oprah.

for those who feel as i—
there are two hopes:

one hope is that you can find
something beautiful,
inside and outside of you,
inside and outside of the many worlds
that surround us,
and hope that you can find laughter and love,
good friends and good food,
a balance, a peace,
and learn to enjoy the good there can be in life and in living,
and share it with others,
and make this world,
all the worlds,
better today than they were yesterday.

the second hope is that there is something good that follows
us after we no longer live in this world.
and if there is,
then i would ask you to do me this one favor:
when you move into the next world,
and after you are settled and you have put away your
socks and toothbrush,
and you have had a little time to
adjust to the place where you will be spending eternity—
after you have done all this,
i ask that you take a walk.
walk to the house of the creator
and knock lightly on her door.
and when he answers,
ask her this:

"Why?"
he will know what you ask.
she will know why you ask.
and you can say to him,
"why did you, omnipotent as all get-out,
create a world where prey and predator is the norm?
maybe you can do nothing with the mess that is now there—
but next time,
please, please, please,
think carefully about
your actions."

if enough of us do this,
maybe next time we can
be the genesis of a world
that is truly,
truly,
heaven on earth.

amen.

the lower level

i've made many attempts to write the following story.
i hope this will be the last.

the first twenty times i began it always opened
with a Doonesbury reference.

i like Doonesbury. read it every day
unless mr. trudeau is on vacation
when they run reruns.
if he takes time off writing it,
i take time off reading it.
tit for tat.

the reference was a conversation
between michael doonesbury and his wife, j.j.,
and they didn't know what to do with their lives
and finally, at a loss as to where they should turn,
exclaim in unison,
"Law School!"

i can relate to that.

my father was a teacher. and somewhere along the line,
he decided to give law school a shot.
a one semester shot.
and that was it.

but that didn't stop him from telling me what he learned that
semester.
and i, like many children on this planet,
loved my father as they loved theirs.
and if our fathers dug coal from the earth,
or drilled cavities from our teeth,
or picked pockets in train stations,
that is something we would wish to do.
and so that seed was planted.
studying law was a worthwhile endeavor.
at least i thought so for quite a few years
until i had forgotten about it and
until it came back to me
after i had diverged up and down many other roads taken…

i was getting close to my thirties when the Logan's Run
idea hit me that i had better do something big right
now because once i crossed into the fourth decade
it would be too late to do anything worthwhile.

my younger brother was already in law school.
and my father's stories came back, and i recalled that
ralph nader was a hero of sorts so i took the LSAT
which i passed and now i was going to be somebody.

yeah.
so i spent three years completing two year's worth
of law school because i was working full time and
going to law school part time…
let me tell you something about that.

i'm usually a pleasant person, get along with co-workers,
tip wait staff 20 percent, and use my turn signals when i drive.

but when i was working full time, and going to law school in the evenings, and then getting home at 9 or ten p.m. and then studying more i was slowly becoming sleep deprived.

sleep deprivation.
i know this isn't news to most of you but for those who just don't know yet, when many of us don't sleep we can be assholes.
now some of you can spend a full nine hours in dream city and you're still pricks. and that means there is really no hope for you.
but if you take a normal person and have them work two full time jobs or have a baby that doesn't sleep for the first three years of life,
it's very easy to cross that line from pleasantness to prickishness.
which explains why so many lawyers get a bad rap…because
many of them deserve it. they are so messed up after three years or more of law school that they want someone to pay for screwing up their lives.
and guess who foots that bill?

my digression rests.

so i was half way through my legal studies.
did you ever decide to do something,
make the commitment,
announce it to the world so you can't back down,
and then when you're in the middle of it
you realize sometimes it's better to be discrete
and not draw a lot of attention to yourself,

just in case you end up not doing what you said?

but i wasn't ready to accept that law school
was not the place for me.

at least i wasn't until one day,
in Torts Class,
the professor called on me to recite the facts
of a case that had taken place in a train station.
so i explained what happened.
and he, as law professors do,
followed with questions.

one thing about law school professors and their questions:
you can't win.
you may think you're winning.
but they're just giving you more rope until they're
ready to pull it tight and leave you hanging in mid-air.

i was doing okay with my replies.
until he asked…
"what was going on at the lower level?"
and i froze.

i freeze a lot in my life.
like a doe in the headlights of god's chevy tahoe

lower level.
lower level?

(i'm thinking to myself.)
the case takes place in a train station.
but i don't remember there being another level.
maybe they were selling tickets?
or baggage…could be they have baggage stored there…
and someone tripped over a bag…

i flipped back and forth through the casebook.

nope. don't recall baggage or tickets.

and i decided to use a hail mary.
hail mary, full of grace, the lord is
driving a tahoe.
and i looked up from my book and said,
"on the lower level? they were selling hot dogs."

okay. i knew i was wrong.
i just didn't know how wrong.
and the laughter that filled the room would have
made jonathan winters smile.
but i wasn't jonathan winters.
and the prof wasn't johnny carson and he
wasn't going to invite me to come up and sit next to
him at the podium.

the prof smiled.
and he said to me,
"when i said lower level, i meant lower *court* level."

yeah.
and my mind went back to the first day of law school when
they prof said, "look to your left…now to your right.
of the three of you, only one will be here at the end."

and i knew then i was going to do something else with my life.
i just wondered if i'd ever find out what it was.

Angel

there is much that happens i do not know about.
things happen that i don't hear about for months—or maybe ever.

so when i heard Angel was in the hospital, she had been there for a while.
in my mind, in my heart, i wished her well and i left it at that.

i went home from work and that evening i thought of Angel again.
and then i decided to write her a note. we we're not best friends, but we had spoken a number of times and i enjoyed the talks we had,
especially when we talked about the theater. we both enjoyed musicals and plays.

i didn't know how she would react to what i would write.
i wanted her to know that somebody who she would not expect to hear from was thinking of her. maybe it would help speed her recovery.

the next day at work i called monica and told her i had a note for Angel.
monica paused.
and then she said Angel had passed away the night before.
i told her i was very sorry to hear that. and i paused.

monica said that if i liked i could give my note to her and she would give it to Angel's family.
and so that's what i did.

>dear Angel:
>hello.
>my name is dave k.

i work at the zoo.
the same zoo you do.
we've talked about the theater and stuff.
and you've been helpful to me.
and heck, that's worth a lot!

anyway.
i heard you are not feeling well.
okay, that may be putting it mildly…

but that's not the point.
the point is
i wanted to write you a note
telling you that even though we didn't
go to school together or
go to the same church,
we are part of the zoo family.
and in the big picture,
we are part of the human family,
and though i can't write a letter to all
my fellow humans who need a word of
support and encouragement and
to let them know that people like me,
just an av guy who hangs out there,
he, that's me,
wants you to know that i'm sending you
good vibes and hoping you heal quickly
and come back to the zoo and
continue doing wonderful work.

(and when you go home,
 you can still go see great plays
and dance and sing and laugh and stuff.
actually you can dance and sing and laugh
at work if you like.)

> okay.
> i've been rambling.
> sending hugs.
> very sincerely,
> dave k., one of the family

that's the end of the note.
but today we are here to celebrate Angel's life.
it was much too short…
but from looking at the photos of her life,
she was a very lucky human being.
she found something that she loved to do,
something that truly made this planet better off
than the world she was born into…
and got to do it pretty much every day of her life…
and *that* is worth celebrating.

voices in my head

dear friends:
this christmas we write to wish you well and
to share some christmas/holiday thoughts.
this year the story begins outside a Goodwill
store on hollywood boulevard.
i was waiting for the Wacko store to open so i
could buy a book called "Toilets of the World"
when a homeless man drifted up to me.
he said, "Would you like to buy this cd player?
Three bucks. I need to get something to eat."

a few weeks earlier i had encountered another
homeless man who asked for money and
instead i bought him a pizza and when i tried
to give it to him he said, "You give that to me
and I'll throw it 'n the street."

so this time, wary though i was, thought
maybe i can get him a sandwich.
"I don't see a restaurant around here—" I said.
"I'd rather have the three bucks."
"What for?"
he gestured toward the Goodwill store,
"They're holding a walkman cassette player
for me. Three bucks."
"Why don't you use the CD player?"
"Cuz I got cassettes."
"Why do you need a cassette player instead
of getting food?"
"I can get food. But the cassettes keeps the
voices out of my head."

i've been approached by a number of
homeless people over the years and that's
something not one of them has said to me.
i thought, hey, if for three bucks i can keep
voices from getting into his head, that's a
pretty good deal.

so i went with him into the store and the lady
behind the counter gave him the walkman
and i paid the three bucks and gave him the
receipt and he thanked me and i figure that's
the best three bucks i've ever spent.

and with that, we wish that you will find the
holidays and the days that follow are happy
ones and hope you are all well and can
experience the good that life can offer.

hitchhiking (there was a time…)

today i passed a woman, standing curbside,
thumb up, looking for a ride and lord knows
what else.
i didn't slow, i didn't pass go, i just continued
on my way
home.

but that's not how it used to be.

i used to walk to the road's edge,
stick out a thumb,
and a car or truck would pull over,
and i'd be off and on my way.

i know people have been hitching
since the first horse was invented and it can be a
great way to get from a to z.
but there are times and places where and when
bad things can happen on the open road when a
lone soul gets into a car and lives are changed forever
and not for the better.

but there was a time…
a magical time…
in the late 60's early 70's when people
shared rides with strangers and it was a good thing,
a communal, spiritual thing…perhaps
the Golden Age of Hitchhiking.

and that was when i, barely thirteen,
began to thumb.

thumb to the Wonderland Mall.
thumb to tim's old man's tow-junk yard
on telegraph in taylor-tucky where i'd
hang out with tim and bill g.
thumb to the roller rink where i'd pretend to like
the coffee i was drinkiing
and bill g. would drink his and smoke marlboros,
newports, winstons.

when i first started i didn't bother tellin' the folks.
they had enough crap to deal with—
why should i add to their burden?
(at times i could be a considerate kid.)

then one day mom found out.
when she did she said to me,
"you be careful and never do it alone"
and then when i thought that was it,
she added,
"and when the car stops—",
i looked at her and she finished with,
"let your friend get in first."
yeah. mom was pretty smart. if there was going
to be trouble, i would be the one to testify.

rabbits

one day bill g. and i were coming back from Wonderland.
some days it got real damn cold, you know?
michigan winters can be a bitch and beyond
and somedays we think no one will stop and we'd
die right there on middlebelt and joy.
and then, a miracle!
a '65 falcon stops twenty feet past us. the light is about

to change and we don't have long so we run to the car.
the passenger window's down and the guy says,
"Both get in the front."

i let bill get in first so i can be a witness
if he pulls a bowie knife from 'neath the seat.
i sit next to bill but before i close the door he's off,
down the road.
"where to?"
"inkster."
He lights a cigarette and bill asks if he's got an extra
and he does. i don't smoke tobacco so i pass.
the guy is quiet. when he comes to a red light he brakes hard
and as he does, an empty bottle of boonesfarm rolls forward
and hits me in the back of my frye's.
light goes green and the bottle rolls to the back.

falcons don't have a lot of power so it's takin' awhile.
the Driver breaks the silence with, "You like rabbits?"
bill looks at me, i at him, we shrug and agree, "yeah."
"that's what i do," he says, "rabbits."
he does rabbits. not sure what that means but hey,
it's sort of a free country,
he jabs his finger backward.
bill and i turn and sitting on the backseat are five rabbits.
and that's when i think i recognize him. he's a big guy,
quiet, but maybe not all there. lenny, i think. lenny got a
driver's license and rabbits and he's giving us a lift. cool.

inkster road arrives and he pulls into a hardee's parking
lot and lets us out.
Thanks, man, we say.
he nods, and takes off before bill can close the door and it
slams shut and he's gone.

gay america

in the suburbs of the auto mobile capital of the world
in the nineteen seventies, being gay was not a good career move.

those that were gay didn't let on.
at least not to me.
sure, there were some who had stereotypical characteristics
associated with being gay
(please don't ask, let's let those sleepy dogs lie…the good news is
many of us have seen the error of our ways. live and let live.)
but in the world and time where i lived if you were gay
you just kept it to yourself.
this time it was mark g. and me thumbing on telegraph
heading to the roller rink,
two fourteen year olds out for adventure,
when the sixty-eight bug pulled over.
mark got in the back, me, the front.
old bugs were cool, the kind of car that maybe someday i could
afford, and the kind of car you turn into a dune buggy.
(there's nothing like a dune buggy in a michigan blizzard.)

so we're talking to the driver…
"where you headin'?" he asked.
"west chicago."
"right, you got a cigarette?"
"no," said mark. neither of us smoked tobacco.

i'm just admiring the car, looking around, and mark's leaning
forward between the seats talking to this guy.

and that's when i see the magnets.
on the dash.

Gay New York
Gay Miami
Gay San Francisco

i think mark saw them about the same time i did.

okay. this is how bad it was then.
if someone was gay and you didn't know about it…
well, to be honest, that was still too gay but what can you do?
i mean, you just don't know about it.
but if someone was gay, and admitted it, advertised the fact
on their dash,
that was scary as hell.

"hey, we'll get out up here," mark said.
"i'm almost there."
"yeah. right. cool, we'll get out here. really," i added

he could read the writing and knew we could too.

he dropped us off and we said thanks and as he drove
away we laughed and thought, shit!, that was close!

and sometimes you think you're in the frying pan and
are lucky to get out, and then find out different
'cause the kitchen is about to burn down.

skillet on the stove

thumbs out, it wasn't long before the Olds 98 pulled up.
fancy car. power windows and doors. heard the power
door locks pop.
mark in back, same routine.
a big-bellied, cigar smoking fifty-year old cat was
behind the wheel.

"how you kids doin'?"
"all right."
"how far you goin', if you know what i mean?"
"west chicago."
"west chicago. ever been to Chicago?"
"nope."
"crazy town. crazy things. crazy women."
(he laughed, we laughed. yeah, crazy women.)
"you guys like women?" he asked.
(i looked back at mark, he at me, we grinned)
"hell yeah!"
"yeah. i bet." his cigar had gone out. he pushed in the lighter.
when it popped he pulled it out and relit the stogie.
"you guys ever get a blow job?"

okay. hey. what fourteen year old is gonna deny having
received a blow job, even if he hadn't? but it's one thing to
be toking a joint with your pals and one of them
brings that up.
but this thing, sitting next to this old fat man,
i just didn't think i wanted to tell him what i did with the
chicks i was dating.
"you know," he continued, "if you were in a room,
and it was black as a moonless night, and someone
was sucking on you, you wouldn't know if it
was a man or woman, you know what i mean?"

yeah, we knew what he meant. he meant he was a
motherfuckin' pedophile and that's not a frying pan,
that's a fucking fire!

"we'll get out here!" mark said.
"yeah here!" i said, backing him up.
the light changed to yellow and the perv accelerated as it
turned red overhead.

"there. there is good. right—" i said as i pointed out the window—
and the car sailed on.
i started to point at the next spot when he pulled to the far left
and into the turn lane and we left telegraph road behind.
fuck!
life can turn on a dime.
and then, before i could really come up with a plan,
he pulled over.
the door locks popped up,
and we scrambled out and before
we could say No Thanks! or Fuck You!
he was gone.
and this time we didn't laugh.
we didn't know how close we came to
the devil only knows what.

hitching.
yeah, we continued to hitchhike after that.
what the fuck do kids know?
too often, not much.

but when my brother was thumbing and some guy
gave him a ride,
pulled a knife,
and stole his pants…

well, in my family, when someone steals your pants,
it's time to take a new road.
one where they don't take your pants.

unnecessary notice

richard brautigan had a lightbulb in his toilet
that was fond of him but i can't say the same.
i did have a job i wasn't fond of and decided to
give it back.
i contacted the HR man and said,
"i don't like this job."
"oh." he said.
"but it's important that i do the right thing."
"which is?"
 "i'm going to give you two weeks' notice."
"what?" he looked down at the papers on his desk. then he said,
"but you've only been here one week."
"yes, that's true."
he said,
"that won't be necessary."

the magic hat

i once met a woman who said
she had a magic hat.
it was a nice hat as far as i could see.
and i told her so.
and then she said,
beneath a mildly knitted brow,
"There are those who do not like this hat.
There are those who I am very close to
that have told me that."

and then the brow became unknitted
and she smiled and said,

"But you know what is also interesting to me
and might be to you, too? There are many more
whom I do not know that love this hat!"
Her smile grew and she was so happy
as she continued:
"People shout to me from passing cars
and trucks and motorbikes, 'I love your hat!'
They stop at my table at the deli,
approach me at the zoo,
even when I am fishing off the pier,
and they say, 'I love your hat!'"

she took a breath.
she looked about the world around her.
and then she looked at me and said,
"But there is one thing they do not know about
this hat and that is it is magical. It's a
magical hat! And when I wear it I know
that whether they like it or not,

deep down they like me.
And I like them.
And I will never part with it."

and then she was gone.
like magic.

and as i looked about for her
something occurred to me…
though i knew very little about her
and the hat—
i did know something she did not.
and that was this:
it was not that the magic was in the hat
but that the magic was in her heart.
that's where the magic lived.
and that is why she had so many friends,
and so much love.

i heard someone call my name

when i was leaving my accounting class i heard someone
call my name.
but i ignored the call because who would know me here? but the
caller called again, and it was ms. mae, co-worker and friend.
we continued down the stairs as she explained she was taking a
theater class.
we stopped to chat and her friend, who had been following her,
departed and as she did, called out,
"love you, mae!"
and mae replied,
clear and loud,
"love you, too!"

and i thought, why don't my accounting mates say such things
when they take leave?
do we not bleed when we are pricked?
and then i recalled that when i told my mates i worked at the zoo,
and had expected the usual—"the zoo! why that's marvelous!"—
instead,
the group got quiet.
and one said,
"not much to do with accounting, does it?"
and he was right.

they were all engaged in banking and finance.
they were employing the knowledge we learned
in our class.
and i…i had watched an elephant swim in a pool on
a rainy fall day,
i looked a giraffe in the eyes and gave him
a pat on his coat,

i watched a markhor lift himself off the ground
and run along vertical walls until he flew past…

and now i was working long hours so i could become
like one of them.
and that was okay.
i could live with that.
but i did hope that one day,
when i was immersed in numbers and balances
and adjustments…
that when the day ended,
and we all filed into the car park,
that before we disappeared behind
tinted windows and headlights,
we would call out to each other,
"love you!"
and would hear in reply,
"love you, too!"

wouldn't that be a nice end
to the work day?

a story of love

One morning he awoke and he felt very happy
and he went to see her and he said,
"I love you."
And she said,
"No you don't."
And he said,
"Oh."
And she said,
"You like me."
And he said,
"Okay."
And then he went away.

The next day he went to her and he said,
"I love you."
And she said,
"Does anyone really know what love is?"
and he didn't know.
And then he went away.

Then one day he knew he did love her
and he went to her and said,
"I love you."
And she said,
"How do you know?"
And he said,
"Because when I hold you I feel balance,
when I touch you I feel peace,
when I kiss you I feel bliss,
when I talk with you the world is perfect,
and when I am not with you
I miss you so much that my heart aches."

"Oh," she said. "Is that what love is?"

And he said,
"Yes."
And she said,
"Then I love you too."
And this time he stayed.

on a mission to a mission to cover a fiscal omission

i went to the mission to return the gift that was given but never paid for. i could see the mission from the freeway where it sat high on a hill.

i exited and went 'round and 'round the streets 'til i found one that ran skyward and that was the one i took. when i arrived i car parked and went up the steps and entered the building and entered a room and stopped short of the woman who sat at a table and i said,

"is this the gift shop?"

she looked around as unsure as i as she looked at the books and pamphlets and simulated Native American trinkets in glass jars and finally determined it was and told me so.

but it was not the gift shop i was looking for.

i had been there before and this wasn't it. i explained to the woman and she said,

"oh, but this is not the mission—this is the museum. the mission is eight miles to the east."

so i left and drove the eight miles to the east to the mission and car parked much further down the hill. i walked up the many steps and onto the porch and through the door.

this was it.

i knew this was the right place as i looked out the window at the Jesus, hands outstretched near a basketball hoop. my brother said when he saw it, "hey, it's the basketball Jesus, 'Pass it to me, pass it to me!"

and here he was still waiting. damn, life can be unfair even to the Christ himself. it sucks being picked last and then when you are no one throws you the ball, even when you're the son of a god.

i took from my pocket the gift that had been given but not paid for and wandered the rows and columns of merchandise that was piled high on wooden tables. around and around the room i went but i could see no gift like the one i had in my hand. so i made a resolution to make an estimation of the gift's value and made a donation into a box that had "donation" written on it and then i left with the gift that had been given and was now paid for.

and now that i had paid it made it less of a gift but it was, after all, the thought that counts, wasn't it?

ameen.

lucky strike

i had been in love before and i did find out it was more than just holding hands. but by then, it was too late. so i decided to fall in love again. but i couldn't see leaving it to chance. there had to be another way. and i had an idea…

at the grocers i asked a woman,

"do you like cats?"

"no," she replied.

"that's fantastic!"

she was puzzled.

i continued, "see, i could have asked you out, you might have said yes, we coulda gone out for a few weeks and then bang!, you spring on me like a jack rabbit coming out of a prickly bush, 'I hate your cats!' but now we've cut to the chase and saved ourselves all that time and trouble."

she thanked me and we went our separate ways.

i could see that internet dating would help me eliminate the cat-haters. at least that was the plan until after three months and one-hundred inquiries, numerous phone calls, and even a few dates, i was no closer to love than when i began.

and now new year's was approaching and i didn't want to spend another one dateless and watching dick clark drop his electric orb on manhattan.

i revisited my list of internet prospects and noticed there was one that resulted in some interesting emails and chats, but just never went anywhere. i emailed and asked her out and, to my surprise, she said sure. i should have been wary and less trusting…she was a young republican, or a middle-aged one and i was sane so there was no way we'd be a match…but i ignored the fact and that's not a good idea, you know?

i wanted to make this a memorable eve and knew what would impress her: live theater. one thing led to another and soon i had two sixth row tickets to The Vagina Monologues.

new year's eve morn arrived and i emailed to find out where to pick her up.
thirty minutes later came the reply.
"dear dave: i can't go."
me: and what do i do with the tickets to the show?
she: take someone else.
me: take someone else?

new year's eve was hours away. how many people have not made plans by now? it could be an insult to even *ask* so late in the game. dick clark here i come. but that's pretty much what one could expect from a middle-aged republican.

i went to the Canon Theater to pick up my tickets hoping to unload them right away and like magic, five minutes later, a man walked to the ticket window and was turned away. "you lookin' for a couple of tickets to the Monologues?" i asked.
"no. just one."
he wanted one.
one.
the show started in ten minutes.
i sold him a ticket cutting my losses in half.
eight minutes more and then, not wanting the ticket go to waste, i entered.

i took my seat next to Mr. One. after a minute of silence i said, "so what's up after the show?"
he said, "i know i bought the ticket from you, but it doesn't mean i want to talk to you."
i said to myself, aloud, "just tryin' to inject some mid-west pleasantries into the evening. shoulda just kept the tickets to my self. but no—"
he stood up and moved to an empty seat in the front row and then had to vacate that when the holder appeared. good riddance.

i enjoyed the show. as my grandfather never said, there's nothing like spending the evening listening to women talk about vaginas.

the crowd began to exit.
but i waited because i'm not a fan of crowds. let the masses thin. kind of an evolutionary thing. and as i sat, i looked about. i looked up, to my right, left. back to the front…and then back to my left.
who is she?
where did she come from?
is her boyfriend in the loo? is her girlfriend getting the car?
it was ten-thirty on new year's eve so what the hell…
i walked over to her and said,
"excuse me, my name is dave and it's new year's eve and i was wondering if you'd like to go across the street to the factory for some cheesecake?"
she looked up at me as i spoke. and then she said, "i don't like cheesecake."

 i presumed that was true. i mean, i can't recall the last time someone lied about cheesecake. fruitcake, sure. but not cheesecake.
so i said, "how about going for a walk?"

she said, "okay."

and so we did.
we walked.
we walked around beverly hills for forty-seven minutes and then, at 11 thirty, she, not wanting to be caught like Cinderella at the midnight hour, said "i've got to go now."

i give her my card,
shook her hand,
and she walked off into the dark, toward a vehicle i could barely make out.
i watched her walk. i wanted to make sure she got there safely.
once she was inside, i got into my car and drove to the beach where i watched the waves come in from japan and thought about my life.
what the hell, it could be worse.

cut to the chase.
we, the non-cheesecake eater, and me, never a big fan of the stuff, have been together for twelve years,
the last half of them married. to each other.

i tried to use the science of ones and zeroes to find the girl of my dreams and came up with zilch.
but one of those zeroes cancelled the date and chance and romance returned.
and i found a woman to love,
and one who loves me,
and best of all,
she likes cats.
go figure.

crazy

i was just dreaming i was walking the halls in high school,
dropping in and out of the offices of guidance counselors
and i said to one,
    "i'm just seventeen
    and i figure i got 4 years of college to sort it out
    and get a job so i can set myself up to do some writing."
and then i woke up
and saw i was fifty seven
and hadn't written anywhere
close to what i wanted to
and i asked myself,
"what does it mean?"
and i answered.
"life is some crazy shit."

AND TWO FOR BEDTIME

ERIN CAT'S TALE

When I think of you, Erin Cat, I think of many good things and many happy days. But what stands out most was the tale that told of your arrival. I did not know you in the beginning; Roslyn told the story to me and this is what I remember.

It began before you were born. You had a sister, I believe. I do not recall her name. Let us call her Lisa.

Lisa Cat: Your Sister

Your sister was not well when she arrived at your adoptive mother's house. But neither of them knew this. Roslyn, your adoptive mother, did sense there was something amiss, and so she took Lisa to the veterinarian. The Good Doctor looked Lisa over thoroughly but could find nothing wrong.

So Roslyn thanked him and brought Lisa home. Over the next few days Lisa's health began to fail. But the failure was very subtle and on a quiet morning after Roslyn had readied for work, she stopped, picked her up and cradled her gently and said,

"Lisa Cat, you do not look yourself. When I am at work today I will call the Good Doctor and schedule an appointment and this evening I will take you to him so you can be made better."

And Lisa Cat purred softly and was reassured. And Roslyn set her down and went to the door and opened it and stepped into the hall and closing it behind her, started down the steps. But then she heard a noise and when she turned back she could see protruding from 'neath the door–a foot.

A Lisa foot. She was stretching so hard, so far, out to her mother.

And Roslyn leaned down and tickled the pad and Lisa giggled and Roslyn said,

"Lisa Cat, Lisa Cat, you be good. And remember, I do love you."

And then Roslyn was off, down the steps and out the door.

That Evening

When Roslyn returned that evening she came up the wooden steps to her door and noticed there was no playful Lisa foot outstretched for her. And when she entered she found no Lisa Cat waiting behind the door. And when she entered the hall there still was no Lisa to be found.

But…when Roslyn entered the kitchen…she found Lisa Cat.

"Lisa Cat," said Roslyn.

"Lisa Cat," she said again.

And she knelt down and said once more.

"Lisa…"

but this time Roslyn was sad.

This time Roslyn knew…

that Lisa Cat was no more.

And she picked up the Lisa Cat in her arms and cradled her so gently. And Lisa lay in the cradle with her arm outstretched. And Roslyn cried. And it was a very sad time in the Roslyn household.

The Good Doctor

The next day the Good Doctor called Roslyn and inquired as to why she and Lisa missed their appointment. And Roslyn told him. And the Doctor was so sorry for he loved animals so much and it still pained him when they left this world for the next. He knew too well what it was to experience the loss of love.

The Arrival

Well, one day, a few months later, the Good Doctor arrived at his office as was his usual. And he set down his briefcase outside the entrance and fumbled momentarily with his keys, found the right one, and inserted it into the lock. But when he turned it, instead of hearing a click of the lock he heard, "meew."

"Meew?" he said to himself. He had never heard the lock say meew. Click or clack or maybe clank. But never "meew." It was such a quiet noise. But it was still a noise and very much out of place. He removed his key, studied the lock and found nothing unusual about it. So again he inserted the key and turned it and, yes, he heard "meew" once more.

But--

this time—

It was coming from the mailbox!

The Good Doctor stepped over to the mailbox and

carefully, slowly, he

lifted…

the…

lid.

A Few Hours Later

A few hours later Roslyn received a telephone call.

"Hello, she said. She did not like telephones but she usually answered when it rang and when she did she was always polite.

"Hello Roslyn. This is the Good Doctor. I hope I find you well on this day."

"Yes, Doctor. I am as well as I can be."

"Yes, I understand. But I have news I would like to share with you. And I believe it is good news."

"Good news is always welcome. Please tell me."

"When I arrived at work this morning I found a surprise waiting for me in the mailbox," he said.

"That's wonderful. What was it?"

"It was a kitten! I found a kitten in the mailbox."

"A kitten in your mailbox? Is it okay?" She was concerned for this kitten and she hadn't even been introduced to it. But that didn't matter. She was like that.

"Yes. She's doing well, thank you very much."

"Why would you have a kitten in your mailbox?" she asked.

"I don't know. It's not a good place to put a kitten. Kittens don't like mailboxes."

"Was it postmarked?" she asked. Since the Good Doctor had already established the kitten was healthy Roslyn wondered if the kitten had been shipped improperly. (She worked for the Post Office and knew that was no way to ship an animal.)

The doctor looked the kitten over but saw no postal markings or stamps of any kind.

"No. The kitten is clean as a whistle."

"Is that a new whistle or used?" she asked.

The doctor had never thought about it. So he guessed and said, "New."

"Good," was Roslyn's reply. "Because if you ever looked inside a used whistle you would see…well, you should just take my word and believe me when I say a used whistle offers no standard for cleanliness."

The doctor could not disagree. Roslyn continued:

"That is good news, Doctor. And I thank you for sharing the news with me. But I must be going now. I hope the two of you get along nicely and--"

"But--" said the doctor, "I was hoping if you had a free moment I could introduce the two of you."

"I really don't have a free moment," which was true because she was so very busy.

The Good Doctor was a good man but he was also very persistent. "If you don't have a free moment I will give you one of mine and you can have it at no cost."

It's not every day that one is given a free moment and Roslyn knew this very well. She decided to accept the doctor's invitation and agreed to a meeting.

After Roslyn hung up the phone she was concerned. She had lost her Lisa Cat just a short time ago and she had loved her so much that she was not prepared to be hurt again. But she had given her word that she would go and her word was as good as gold.

The Walk

Roslyn lived a short walk from the veterinarian and so she decided to get it over with. Sometimes it's best to do just that. If there is something you don't want to do you should do it and then it will be done.

As she walked past the homes she noticed that many had already put up their Halloween decorations: all oranges and blacks and yellows. And then Roslyn had a strange thought:

"I've had black cats, and gray ones, stripe-ed and calicos, and tawny-colored too. And I loved them all. But I have never had an orange cat. I don't know why. I guess I was never meant to have an orange cat. Besides, I much prefer the gray and black ones or even the Russian Blues. But I will pass on the orange, thank you very much."

This was sort of a peculiar thing, not wanting an orange cat. But we humans are an unusual tribe and sometimes you just have to accept us for what we are.

She entered the Good Doctor's shop and greeted the receptionist and then sat down patiently.

And waited.

Not long.

And thought to herself, "Yes. A brown kitten would be nice."

And then the Good Doctor appeared in the doorway and he beckoned to her. And she rose and thought as she walked toward the door, "Or even a white one. But not an orange kitten. It's nothing personal of course."

She peered into the room. There was no kitten to be found.

"I'm sorry, Doctor, but I don't see…"

And then she stopped talking. Just like that. In the middle of her sentence. And she just stared at the doctor.

And there he stood, holding in his hands—a mailbox.

The Doctor smiled a wee smile and then looked down at the mailbox and nodded and said, "It's the only place she feels safe."

Roslyn stepped slowly, toward, the, box.

And then she slowly reached out,

and carefully,

and slowly,

lifted

the

lid.

And there…

for all the world to see, that is, if the world could have fit in that little office they would have seen…

the brightest orange kitten that would ever be!

It was radiant!

It was phosphorescent!

And Roslyn was wide-eyed.

She didn't know what to do.

She didn't know what to say.

But the kitten knew what to do.

The kitten knew what to say.

And that was…

"meeew."

Roslyn looked at the Doctor who looked at her and then he smiled a wee smile and then looked back at the kitten and Roslyn looked back at the kitten and then, well, she did the polite thing because if you recall she was, after all, a very polite person.

"Hello," she said.

And at that the kitten leapt almost straight up from the mailbox and landed on the Doctor's head.

"What a jumper!" said the Good Doctor. But the doctor was wearing a rug on his head and it began to slip so the kitten quickly leapt to Roslyn's shoulder. And there it sat.

And Roslyn looked at the kitten from the corner of her eye and thought, "This kitten is such an orange that she would put a pumpkin to shame. The only thing missing is the stem coming out of her head."

Of course Roslyn would never say this aloud. It would not be polite to do so.

"Well, what do you think?" asked the Good Doctor.

"I think—"

and the kitten gave her a lick on her face and then curled up and proceeded to sleep on Roslyn's shoulder and purr oh-so-contentedly.

And Roslyn laughed lightly for she did not want to disturb the kitten.

This kitten was oh so cute. How could she turn her away?

But still…

To the doctor she said, "I was hoping she was—"

and then she looked at the little fluffball of orange and finished with

"—ready to go home with me today."

"Why of course," said the Doctor.

And that is how you, Erin Cat, arrived and shared many, many happy years with Roslyn.

And you enjoyed the quiet, the solitude.

And all was well, even after your brother arrived.

But was a tale of a different color.

In Closing

And you were a comfort to her.

And you were there for each other.

And you were as a good a daughter cat as she could have wished for.

And though you are gone you will always be there.

And though you will always be missed you will always be remembered.

Good Night

Good night, Erin.

Good night, Love.

Good night,

and sweet dreams.

The Chocolate Heart:
A Tale Of Love . . .
About The One I Love . . .
For The One I Love . . .

Once upon a rhyme, long before a rose was to be read, or a violet would ever feel blue, there was a small village on the earth's equator. And in the village the people were very proud of their weather. It was warm in the winter and hot in the summer and almost all the people worshipped the sun because it made their coffee plants grow to be as big as oak trees. And they loved their coffee.

If you were paying attention you will notice I said, in the previous paragraph, that "almost" all the people worshipped the sun. And that was true. But there was one who did not.

And that was a little girl.

And her name was Rozamine.

Now Rozamine learned to enjoy the flavor and aroma of coffee as much as the next child or even the one after that. But there was something missing—there was little joy in her life. All the village folk could see it in her eyes as they picked the coffee beans in the fields.

"What troubles you little one, why do you despair?" asked her family and friends.

But she did not reply for she did not know the answer to the question. And they all knew she knew not the answer for if she did she would have told them because she was very direct. Some even considered this to be a serious character flaw but those people were numbskulls and it is best to ignore a numbskull if you meet one.

One day, when Christmas was nearing, all the children gathered in the village square so they could speak of all the wonderful gifts the Bear god would bring. As they began to laugh and frolic and look through the Sears catalogue, they noticed that Rozamine was not with them.

And this made them sad. "We must do something about Rozamine. She is so unhappy!" said one.

"Oh, but not always," said another. "During the harvest she loves being in the fields and 'neath the sun that turns her skin the color of the beans and not one of us is happier." And this was true. But what did it mean? How could Rozamine be so happy one season and so sad another?

No one knew. And so they all sat down and cried. So sad was this village.

While the village children wept Rozamine was at home in her room sitting by the window. She was knitting a blanket of wonderful colors. Her mother entered and saw what her daughter was doing but she asked anyway:

"And what is this my little petunia brain? You are making a blanket when the temperature never drops below eighty degrees? So foolish you are. It must come from your father's side." And then her mother left.

Suddenly, from where to this day we do not know, a cool breeze came in from the window. Rozamine stopped knitting her blanket so she could knit her brows. And then the breeze grew colder and colder and Rozamine had to put on the blanket that she was knitting. And then she did a strange thing that they still talk about in the village 'round. Rozamine went downstairs and out the door and walked to the center of town where all the children were still weeping. But when they saw her, they stopped. And then right before them she lay on the ground and put her arms overhead and stretched her legs out before her and then began to move her legs and arms back and forth. At first the children were amused.

(Children are like that.) Then one of the adults came over to see what was going on. When the adult saw her he yelled, "Yellow fever! The plague! Run for your lives!" (Adults are like that.) And everyone panicked.

But Rozamine was not concerned with the silly people. She stood and looked at the ground where she had lain. It didn't look like it was supposed to. She didn't know what it *was* supposed to look like, but she knew it didn't look like she thought it should.

And then she had a vision. (It's okay to have visions once in awhile.) She packed her bags and took a bright yellow Checker cab to the station where she boarded a train heading north out of town.

North. For three days and three nights. And at every new town (not the old ones, only the new) she would disembark and lie on the ground and move her arms and legs. Sometimes people would scream and run and other times they would throw money (it's often easier to throw money at what we don't understand, you know) and every once in a while a few could see she had a vision and they would respect that and just let her be.

And the children who were near would be amused until an adult would scream "Plague" and cause plenty of trouble for the town. Once in a while the town would calm down and realize what numbskulls they were and then they would pass a jug or spittoon or mixing bowl around to raise money so Rozamine could continue her journey to wherever she was going. (Most of the folk were just glad to see her go. They weren't concerned as to where that might be.)

On the third day and moving into the third night Rozamine was sitting patiently in her seat. She was alone now, but for the conductor and the engineer. Which was okay with her. The cool breeze she had felt in her village was growing stronger every day, which was good, but it was not enough.

Until.

Until the conductor came into the car and sat across from her and told her this was the last stop. And he added that if she did not get off now the train would be turning around and going back to her village. And she wasn't ready for that.

So she grabbed her blanket and at the door she turned to thank the conductor because she was a polite child. She lifted her arm to shake his hand but lost her balance and fell out the door and into a big, pile of fluff. The conductor called out, "Are you okay, child?"

"Yes," was her reply. And then she asked what was the fluff she had fallen into?

"Why, that is snow!" said the man.

"Snow? What is it good for?" asked Rozamine.

"No good, if you ask me. It snarls traffic and makes noses and feets cold. It's very disruptive and we could do without it."

"I don't know about that," said Rozamine, "It looks wonderful to me."

"Wonderful?" said the conductor. "That's the first time I ever heard anyone say that."

Rozamine thanked the man and taking her blanket she walked away. She walked to the center of town and where Main Street met State Street she lay down in the intersection and began to move her arms and legs about.

And the people stopped.

Car drivers and bus drivers and truck drivers and pedestrians all gathered around. Some were angry and cursed. Others smiled. Many did not know what to do. But she ignored them all and continued to move her arms and legs. And when she felt she was done she got up and stepped carefully back.

There was a loud gasp! Such a surprise did they see. There, in the snow before them, was the most beautiful snow angel they had ever seen. (And the only one, too, because this was the first. But it is widely accepted that no one has ever made a prettier snow angel than the one that Rozamine made at the intersection of Main and State that beautiful winter's day.)

And then she made a snowball and threw it at the newsgirl. The newsgirl picked up some snow and made a snowball and threw it back. Soon the whole town was throwing snowballs. And when Rozamine stopped they stopped. And she walked into the hardware store and purchased two butter knives and some string and then walked down to the pond.

The whole town followed.

And then she strapped the knives to her feet and jumped onto the ice.

"Look out! You'll fall in!" they all exclaimed because none of them had ever ventured beyond the water's frozen edge.

But she didn't fall in or down. Around and around she went. And she did flips and leaps and spirals and it was a wonderful sight to see. Soon others were racing to the hardware store where they purchased butter knives and strapped them to their feet. And they skated into the night.

And when they were tired they stopped and Rozamine went to the Robert McCloskey Inn and rented a room. And so did everyone in town. The whole town was staying at the Robert McCloskey Inn. And before they all went to their rooms Rozamine invited them all into the dining room where she made large pots of steaming coffee (which they had never had before). And they loved it. It was wonderful. And for some of the adults she added Frangelico and they were grateful for the rest of their lives.

The next day the people of the town declared a holiday in Rozamine's honor. No one went to work. They spent the day skating. Some of the people took their skates to the highest hill in town and skated down it. No one had ever had this much fun in winter before. And all of the townspeople were very happy.

And so was Rozamine.

Christmas passed and she enjoyed the cold and snow very much. But then toward Spring she began to miss the summer. But to her surprise the sun began to come out more often and it grew warmer. But then she grew alarmed. "Where is all the snow going? I do miss the sun but I miss the snow even more."

"Do not worry," she was told. "We have many seasons in this town. Winter will return."

This was very reassuring to Rozamine.

For those of you who remember, this is the tale of love. And this is how that part of the story came to be.

One summer Rozamine took a trip back home to visit. She had a very nice time but eventually had to return to the town in the north. When she was on the train she met the same conductor who had been so helpful the first time she had left the village. She also remembered how he had not one good word to say about snow and she wondered if he still felt the same way.

"No," he said. "I do like snow angels and snowball fights and skating on ice."

"I agree," she said. "But there is one thing that is missing."

"What is that?" he asked.

"During the long winter nights when I go home alone it gets very cold from my toes to my nose."

Rozamine had never said these words before but now she knew what they meant. And she knew something needed to be done.

When she returned to her home in the north she spent all her days and nights trying to find an answer to this problem. She tried adding more blankets to her bed, more coal to the fire, more insulation to the attic but nothing seemed to work.

Then she had a vision. The next day she went downstairs and

sat on her front porch in the cold and waited.

And waited.

And waited.

Soon people would stop by and ask her why she sat on her porch day and night in all kinds of weather.

"Because when the winter day is long and I am home alone my nose and my toes get so very cold." The few who stopped by offered suggestions but none were what she was looking for (though some were quite inventive!) As months went by and the news of the vigil began to travel, it was not long before there were thousands of people lined up for miles so they might offer her suggestions.

She sat there for ten years, that's how determined she was. And just like the train that was running out of track when she found her answer, there stood a young man at the end of the line. He carried a small suitcase and a small box wrapped in very becoming paper. She could see him sticking his head out of line so that he could better see her. And then he would pop back into line and be hidden from view. But just when she had almost forgotten about him he would stick his head out again. And always he would smile.

As the line came to an end she kind of got used to him standing there. The line had been moving rather slowly. She knew the man had been there for at least three weeks. But since he was at the end of the line she was in no hurry to have it end because she felt when it did that there would no answer to how she could keep her toes and her nose warm.

But finally, before she knew it, there he was, standing before her, the end of the line.

"You are the end of the line," she said.

He looked behind himself to make sure she was right and she was. (Later he would find out she was maybe not always right but she was never wrong.) He turned back to her and bowed as gracefully as nature would allow and said, "You are quite right. All this time I have been waiting for you, you are all I have seen, you and the back of the gentleman's head who was in front of me."

"That must have been trying for you. How long have you been standing in line?"

"Ten years," he said.

"But that is impossible. If you had started out so long ago you would have been here long before now."

"True. But every time someone else got in line I got behind them."

"But why?" she asked.

"Because I wanted to be alone with you."

"Well, then, if every time someone got into line and you got behind that person, then you would have seen the backs of many heads by now."

"In theory, yes. And that is how it was for the first six years. But after that, it just happened a man appeared who had the same intentions as I. So for four years we have been trying to stand behind each other. It is finally at this moment I have succeeded." He smiled.

"And how did you manage that?"

"I told him that in a previous life you and I were once married and this troubled him."

"Why did this trouble him?" she asked.

"Over these many years we have become good friends. The more I told him about our children—"

"Our Children?!" She was quite surprised to hear this.

"Yes. And our dogs and cats and pigs, both pot-bellied and the pink ones…well, he decided he could not be the one to break up such a happy home."

"Do you think I approve of you being dishonest in order to be alone with me?" she asked.

"Yes."

"And how do you justify such a thing?"

"Because I love you."

"How can you love me? You do not know anything about me."

"That is not true. I know that when the wind blows through your hair I can smell roses in the air."

"That's just my shampoo," she said matter of factly.

"I love everything about you. Your eyes and what they see. Your hands and the way you move them. Your voice as I heard it softly on the wind. So soothing, peaceful. There is so much that I love about you that—"

"Wait. Before you continue, can you tell me how I am to keep my toes and nose warm on those long winter nights?"

"Is there anything you cannot learn?" he asked.

"No. Nothing," she said.

"Then if you can learn to love me then I can keep you warm on those cold winter nights."

"No. There are only two things that I love. There will be no more."

"And what two things are those?"

"I love only making angels in the snow and sipping coffee in the mornings and evenings."

"If I could offer you something else that you could love, other than me, would you try?"

"I see no reason to."

"Please. I have waited ten years to spend this moment with you. If you do but this little thing I will ask nothing more of you and I will be on my way."

"Ok. I will try this," she said.

"And if you love it then you will spend some time with me and see if you can learn to love me?"

"Yes," she said.

And with that he set down his suitcase and handed her the box he had under his arm."

"What is this?" she asked.

"Please open it."

She opened it and found in the box a heart as dark as a jaguar's spots.

"And what am I do with this?"

"Take a piece and taste it."

She broke off a small piece and put it into her mouth and it began to melt. Such a taste, such a feeling. It was the most wonderful thing in the world! It was even better than snow angels or coffee in the morning or coffee in the evening.

"I love this," she said. "I love this more than anything! What is it?"

"They call it chocolate."

She looked at him, he at her. And then he said as he produced a ring from his vest pocket, "Will you marry me please?"

"Forever?" she asked.

"Yes. Forever."

She was about to accept when she remembered it was not Sunday. She could only accept if it were a Sunday. "It's not Sunday."

"That's true in most places," he said, "but here we have a special month. You've heard of a month of Sundays?"

She nodded.

"That's what we have. And every day is Valentine's day. Is your nose a little cold?"

She nodded once more. "And my toeses, too."

So he took her hand and married her that very same day.

And though her nose and her toeses did occasionally get cold they were not cold for very long.

The End.

(inspired by roslyn daguanno)

PS. as linda ellerbee said, And so it goes.

there was going to be a third story for bedtime but i have decided it will be published separately.

it's called "Where Does Time Go?" and has wonderful illustrations by Erika L. Chan.

Please be kind and enjoy life.

Peace.

the bus waits for no one

so this book was supposed to come to an end by now
but before it does, and before i do,
i have a bit more to add.

i have been writing this book for over fifty years. that's a long time, a lot of effort, a lot of living, dying, laughing and crying, to arrive at the pages you hold in your hands.

i asked three wise friends to look it over before i was ready to set it free and they said they liked what they read. but one did say she did not see how "And Two For Bedtime" was connected to the rest of the book.

i told her, "connected or not, there is a bus out there with my name on it. i do not know when or where, but when it comes for me, i will no longer be. the bus will not wait and neither can i. so i have put into this all that is ready and hope it works. if i wait another day it might be too late."

remember, no one but gods and vampires escapes the bus.

www.ingramcontent.com/pod-product-compliance
Lightning Source LLC
Chambersburg PA
CBHW070544300426
44113CB00011B/1785